*f*RESH *f*LOWER
*a*RRANGING

fresh flower arranging

Kate Morris   Andreas Neophytou   William Bacon

CHARTWELL
BOOKS, INC.

A QUINTET BOOK

Published by Chartwell Books
A Division of Book Sales, Inc.
110 Enterprise Avenue
Secaucus, New Jersey 07094

This edition produced for sale in the U.S.A.,
its territories and dependencies only.

ISBN 0-7858-0099-9

This book was designed and produced by
Quintet Publishing Limited
6 Blundell Street
London N7 9BH

Senior Editor: Laura Sandelson
Creative Director: Richard Dewing
Designer: James Lawrence
Editor: Lydia Darbyshire
Photographer: Nick Bailey

Typeset in Great Britain by
Central Southern Typesetters, Eastbourne
Manufactured in Singapore by
Bright Arts Pte Limited
Printed in China

CONTENTS

INTRODUCTION

Flowers have been used for centuries to decorate and perfume houses. Bringing cut flowers into our homes adds color and scent, it is true, but the flowers add an extra dimension that cannot be created with soft furnishings and accessories – they bring with them a sense of life and growth, making a room come alive. Think how welcoming flowers are when you find an elegant arrangement in a hotel lobby or a simple posy on a restaurant table. Having fresh flowers in your home, even if only on weekends or during holidays, will instantly cheer you, your family and friends, and will make your home much more welcoming.

Each season brings a fresh range of flowers and foliage to use around the house, and whether you wish to create a formal arrangement for a celebration or simply add some fresh flowers to a room, there is always something new to try. You can make the most of special features in any room with a carefully chosen and arranged selection of flowers – empty fireplaces, tabletops, bedside cabinets, vanity shelves in bathrooms, and kitchen tables are all ideal places to feature an arrangement of colorful flowers.

There is a lot of mystique surrounding the skill of flower arranging, but, with practice, you will find that your eye soon develops so that you create increasingly effective arrangements. Once you have chosen a group of flowers and foliage that you think will go well together, consider where the arrangement will be placed and which container you plan to use. It is then a matter of creating a shape that suits all three, and that shows off the flowers and foliage to their best advantage. Some people find this a very simple process; others have to take their time, and may make what they believe to be mistakes along the way. Keep a record of arrangements that catch your eye, and try to think why they attract you – is it the choice of colors? The container? Or the particular flowers that have been used? Dramatic arrangements in hotel lobbies, for example, are great inspiration for smaller-scale arrangements in your own home. Use books, magazines, fabrics, and gardens to give you ideas of colors and shapes, too, but don't be afraid to experiment – you will soon get to know what works and what does not.

MATERIALS AND EQUIPMENT

A few simple tools are all that one needs to begin flower arranging. The more specialized items can be added as you become more adventurous in your design. Flower arranging need not involve a large investment – containers, for instance, can usually be found in most homes in all shapes and sizes. A good pair of flower scissors or small pruning shears, a sharp knife, a watering can, and floral foam are some of the basic implements discussed in this chapter, and are recommended as valuable aids to technique.

Choosing Your Flowers

Choosing the flowers, selecting two or three stems that complement or contrast with each other in terms of color or shape, is often the starting point of an arrangement. You will notice that many of the compositions in this book use a minimal number of stems very effectively because they can often be divided to provide a number of pieces for the arrangement from the one stem, so be careful not to buy or cut too many.

FLOWERS CLOCKWISE FROM
TOP LEFT:

carnation, prairie gentian, freesia, aster, lily, chrysanthemum, gerbera, throatwort, iris, alstroemeria, delphinium, mimosa, gentian, liatris, centaurea thistle, calla lily, rose, and spider chrysanthemum.

If you try to use more than is needed, you can end up with a cluttered and over-packed arrangement in which the flowers do not have a chance to show off their delicate shapes. Also, bear in mind the container you plan to use and the overall effect you wish to create. Is it to be a formal arrangement with a well-defined shape, or a more casual selection of flowers in a container? Where will you position the flowers? What other colors are there in the room? All these factors need to be thought about when you are choosing.

When you visit your local florist you often rely on their help and expertise in selecting the best from the bunch, but it helps to know exactly what you are looking for. The florists know how long the stems have been in the shop, and they may be keen to sell you flowers that are not very fresh and that will not last very long once you get them home, so be very observant.

Look carefully at the display, selecting stems on which the flowers have firm petals and healthy-looking foliage. Some of the flowers should be open, but try to get stems with coloring buds, too, because this will help your arrangements last longer. Buds not showing any signs of color are less likely to open. However, spring flowers such as tulips are an exception to this rule, because they last for a relatively short time once opened. Ask the florist to wrap the flowers well so that the full

length of the stems is supported with the paper, which also helps avoid undue evaporation.

Once you get the flowers home, trim about 1½ inches off the bottom, ideally while holding the stem under water to prevent air-locks from forming. Then set the flowers in deep, tepid water for a refreshing drink. This is known as conditioning. If the heads are hanging heavy, rewrap the flowers in paper for support before steeping them in water. Leave them in a cool, dark place until you are ready to use them.

Many flowers can be grown in your own garden to be cut and brought inside. Cut them early in the morning while the air is still cool, and keep the stems as long as you can. Carry a bucket of tepid water with you so that the stems can go immediately into the refreshing water for a drink. Only cut as many as you need so that more blooms will be there for another day.

When you are ready to arrange the flowers, you can recut the stems to the length you need. Once you have finished arranging the flowers, check that they have sufficient water, and place them out of direct sunlight, away from heaters or open fires and out of drafts. Top up the water daily, especially if the container is small, and replace with fresh water where possible every two to three days. If you can, move the flowers to a cooler spot overnight and they will last even longer.

Choosing Your Foliage

Although foliage is most commonly thought of as the green leaves that form the background on which to display flowers, the different colors and shapes of foliage material, available both in gardens and at the florist, can make a wonderful arrangement on their own. In fact, the key to many of the designs in this book is the use and variety of foliage – if you look carefully, you will see that many feature very little in the way of true flower stems, the color and texture being provided by the variety of the foliage material.

FOLIAGE CLOCKWISE FROM
TOP LEFT:

needlefern, heather, rosemary, dragon's claw willow, ken grass, ivy, bay, timothy grass (cattails), bear grass, euonymus 'Emerald and Gold', sugar pine, greater bamboo, eucalyptus, beech (preserved in glycerine), tingiringi gum, and laurel.

Do not make your selection of foliage as an afterthought; it should be chosen when you select the flowers. The foliage is there to complement the flower stems and the overall shape of the arrangement. Keep a watchful eye on your garden and hedges as the year progresses. Even the colors of evergreen trees will change as the year turns, and this provides an ever-changing palette for you to use. Look at the reverse side of the leaves, too, as the color and texture variations can be used to add depth to your arrangements.

Select and treat lengths of foliage in a similar way to cut flowers, examining the stems carefully and checking for falling leaves before you buy. Trim the stems by about 2 inches and set them in tepid water for a drink while you prepare to put together the arrangement. Most woody stems will benefit if you make a long diagonal cut to increase the surface area in contact with the water. When you cut lengths from the garden, bear in mind that it will affect the overall growing shape of your plant, so take care to cut stems from all over. As with cutting flowers, try to do so early in the day, while the plant is still cool and damp from the nighttime temperatures.

Always remove leaves that are below water level in a vase or on that part of the stem that is to be pushed into floral foam because they can damage the foam and impair support of the stem. Leaves are ideal hiding places for the bacteria that will affect the life of your arrangement. Do not discard lengths of foliage – make the most of a stem by cutting the length you need close to the next set of leaves to create a new top. Pieces without true growing tips can be used for filling in and in places where the tops will not be seen in silhouette. Remember to keep the foliage that comes with the flowers, too, because these leaves can often be used to enhance the arrangement and fill it out.

Many varieties of foliage plants and grasses can be grown in your own garden, ready to cut when you need them. However, if you do not have access to a wide variety of foliage, ask your florist to look out for a wider selection. There is often a huge choice available, and many florists will be willing to buy exotic or out of the ordinary stems for you, particularly if you are preparing arrangements for a special occasion.

Vase Life

There are many ways of prolonging the life of your flowers and foliage once you have arranged them. The most destructive agent is bacteria, which is why it is so important to use clean tools and containers at all times. This is also why foliage is stripped from stems that are to stand in the reservoir of water feeding the arrangement, because these can encourage microbiological growth. Additives can be used to inhibit bacterial growth. Some commercial flower foods include mild disinfectants in addition to nutrients, or you could add a mild solution of bleach or disinfectant or a soluble aspirin (half a tablet to 2½ cups).

Choosing Containers

Just as the selection of the flowers and foliage should be taken together, so the choice of a container should be thought about when you are buying or cutting for an arrangement. The color and shape of a container can enhance the overall design and balance of your flowers, just as it can overpower the flowers if the color or size is wrong.

Any receptacle that can hold water or that can be adapted to hold water can be used for flower arranging. Floral foam and various other items can be used to help the arrangement along (see page 14), opening up a whole realm of possibilities. Plates, jam jars, baskets, egg cups, storage jars, cooking and serving dishes – the list of potential containers for flower arranging is only as limited as your imagination. I, for example, am a firm believer in buying pitchers, which come in endless sizes, shapes, and colors, and which can always be cleaned thoroughly after flower arranging and used on the table again.

If you have a vase you find impossible to use, I hope you will find an arrangement in this book to try. The big green jar used for Sunny Day (page 31), for example, had been collecting dust and was used occasionally for gladioli until I was shown how to use it more creatively.

If the color of the container is wrong, try spraying with car paint to transform it into a more sympathetic color. This also works on jam jars, and is an excellent way of acquiring gold and silver containers for festive arrangements. When the container is used as a base that will not be seen after the arrangement is finished, plastic trays or disposable plates and dishes are ideal; and, if you are making the arrangement as a gift, it is much easier to use a disposable container or tray than to have to retrieve your vase or basket after the arrangement has finished. Wreaths are another example of arrangements in which the bases are not seen. The frame or ring actually becomes the skeleton of the arrangement, and so cannot be used again. All the wreaths featured in this book use a wire moss frame as a base.

As you look through this book, you will see that we have used a wide variety of containers, and the examples should help you think about the overall proportions and balance of the designs when you come to choose your own.

Whatever container you use, it must be absolutely clean. If necessary, rinse it out with a bleach solution before you use it to be absolutely sure, because bacteria can remain for some time and then affect your next arrangement.

Potential containers for flower arranging are limited only by your imagination.

Tools

As you progress through the projects in this book, you will find that several tools will be invaluable; you may already have them to hand. They make the job of preparing and cutting flower and foliage stems easier, and this, in turn, will make the putting together of an arrangement more straightforward. Starting with the correct tools for the job is one way in which flower arranging can be more enjoyable.

CLOCKWISE FROM
TOP LEFT:

silver wires, floral foam, frog, glass marbles, fine stub wires, reel wire, floral tape, thicker gauge stub wires, glass marbles, stem tape, small pruning shears, florist's scissors, sharp knife, florist's ribbon, German pins, clay pebbles, and floral foam.

- **Florist's scissors**, which are specially designed for cutting stems and wires, are sharp, light, and easy to handle.
- **Small pruning shears** are essential for cutting thicker branches and woody stems. Look for some lightweight ones because average garden versions can be heavy.
- **Sharp knife**. You will need a long blade for cutting and trimming floral foam, as well as for slitting and trimming stems.
- **Watering can**. Choose one with a long spout designed for indoor plants so that you can get right to the heart of an arrangement.

- **Plant spray**. Many plants can take up moisture through their petals and leaves, and benefit from the occasional light spray with water.
- **Deep bucket**. Use one that has side handles or one with the central handle removed so that stems are not damaged while they are drinking.

Just as you keep utensils exclusively for use with food, so should you keep your flower arranging tools just for that purpose. Always clean them meticulously after use to ensure that bacteria cannot become established and then transferred to the freshly cut stems you bring home.

Materials

The nuts and bolts of an arrangement that support the flowers and foliage are many and varied, though most are hidden in the finished work. Although it is sometimes possible to rely simply on the support of other stems in the container, arrangements will usually benefit from some help. All these items should be available through your local florist or garden center.

- **Floral foam**. The dry blocks need to be cut to size then thoroughly pre-soaked in tepid water before use – you can do this while the flowers and foliage are conditioning. There should be space around the block for additional water because it needs to be kept moist. It cannot be reused successfully.
- **Floral tape, frogs, and fixing putty**. These items are used to hold floral foam in position in containers. The fixing putty is extremely sticky and resilient; it is also useful for securing wires and attaching containers to stands.

- **Stem tape**. This green, paper-based tape sticks to itself and is used to cover wires on stems.
- **Reel wire and stub wires**. You will need both kinds of wire to support flower heads or to encourage flowers and foliage to bend in the right direction for your arrangement. Stub wires come in pre-cut lengths, and both kinds come in a variety of gauges for use with different weights of stem.
- **Silver wire**. This very fine, bright metal wire is used for delicate flowers. It is usually sold in bundles of pre-cut lengths, similar to stub wire.
- **German pins**. These pre-formed pins, a bit like hairpins, are used to hold materials like mosses in position in bases or on wreaths.
- **Marbles, chicken wire, clay pebbles, and floral jelly** are all used to hold stems in position when floral foam may not be appropriate.

If it is possible to reuse materials, always make sure that they are left clean for next time or all your hard work could be spoiled by bacteria.

ROUND ARRANGEMENTS

Flower arrangements come in many shapes and sizes, and their suitability for different locations will often depend on this. There are many occasions when you will want to create a display of flowers to be viewed from all sides, and we have designed 10 round arrangements with this in mind.

Just a quick look through the variety of sizes and styles of design in this chapter will reveal the range of containers we have used. There is no need to stop at vases – we have used a drinking glass and an old teapot for a bit of whimsy, as well as pre-formed floral foam rings and moss rings on which to base arrangements.

Making a Round Arrangement

Whatever the size or style of the finished arrangement, you will want the flowers to look good from all angles, which means careful preparation and assembly. Although this may sound time consuming, the ground rules can be reapplied time after time, and as you get accustomed to them you will become quicker and more proficient at building up the perfect all-around arrangement. By following the step-by-step method for the table posy you will see how the round shape is built up, and you will repeat this same method for all the other com-

positions that use floral foam as a base.

Circlets and wreaths obviously require different skills, and there are examples of these for you to copy, too. Remember that you can adapt the materials to the flowers and foliage that are available, but you should keep the proportion of flower to foliage shown, and make sure that the range of colors, the sizes of flowers, and the overall scale are as similar as possible. Follow these simple rules and your own version should be just as successful as the ones illustrated.

*p*URPLE *p*OSY

There are many occasions when a table needs a central posy such as this. This style is suitable for a dining table because the low dome of flowers and foliage will not distract the eye. To make it more special, perhaps for an evening party, you could add fine flower candles, which would press easily into the floral foam base. If you do plan to make a flower arrangement for the table, be careful to select scentless flowers, or the perfume will affect your guests' enjoyment of the food!

This step-by-step design follows a basic pattern that can be used time and time again.

YOU WILL NEED:

Small, low dish
Floral foam with frog, fixing putty, and floral tape
2 stems eucalyptus
1 stem box
1 sprig heather
8 stems cornflowers
15 scabious
3 stems baby's breath

1 Prepare the dish by securing a square of pre-soaked floral foam with a frog stuck to the base of the dish with fixing putty and taped over the top with floral tape. Trim off the top corners to make a rounded shape. The foam extends about 3 inches above the rim of the dish. Place nine even lengths of eucalyptus around the outside edge of the block to make a circle. Turn the dish to make sure it is even all around. This will be the circumference of the finished arrangement.

2 Moving up the block, evenly space six more pieces of eucalyptus, slightly shorter than the first pieces, then arrange three pieces of eucalyptus on the top of the block, so that they come up rather than out. Turn the dish and check that the shape is even all around before echoing this skeleton with box foliage.

3 Continuing the nine, six, three pattern of the eucalyptus and box, add some color with the heather, working around the container as you go. Fill in alternate spaces with cornflowers at all levels of the arrangement. Use buds as well as open flowers, although only the open flowers will provide color, so these need to be spaced evenly.

4 Starting at the top of the arrangement, position the scabious flowers. These will add depth as well as color, and they need to be placed at the top and middle of the arrangement. Turn the dish as you move down, adding the scabious as you go. Cut the stems so that they are slightly shorter than the surrounding foliage.

5 For a final touch and to soften the overall shape, add small sprigs of baby's breath to any spaces in the arrangement, making sure that they are even all around and that the overall silhouette is smooth.

CRYSTAL CONTRAST

This small, compact arrangement is a perfect way of showing off both delicate flowers and a fine piece of glassware. It would be ideal for a side table when you are entertaining, or you could place it on the drinks tray when you take the glasses around to your friends. You could use baby's breath instead of lily-of-the-valley.

YOU WILL NEED:

Large wine glass
Floral foam to fit top
12 stalks bear grass
5 trails ivy
1 stem eucalyptus
4 lily-of-the-valley leaves
1 piece butcher's broom
10 pink freesias
7 salmon-pink sweet peas
7 mauve alstroemerias
13 lilies-of-the-valley

Cut the floral foam so that it fits like a plug in the glass, and so that it goes into the glass to a depth of about 1 inch and sits 3 inches above the rim. Make an outline with bear grass, remembering to turn the glass and look at it from all sides so that the pieces are evenly spaced around the entire block. Add the ivy, with one trail extending down on one side, the eucalyptus around the top section, and the lily-of-the-valley foliage around the center. Distribute small pieces of butcher's broom evenly around the arrangement. Evenly space the freesia blooms around the entire shape, then place sweet peas and alstroemerias in the gaps. Position the lily-of-the-valley stems to add the final touch.

CIRCLET

A straw hat decorated with fresh flowers conjures up images of summer weddings and celebrations. To prepare the stems, follow the wiring instructions for the corsage on page 56. Have all the stems, flowers, and foliage ready before you start to put the circlet together, and, when it is finished, mist it with water and keep in a cool place until you need it.

YOU WILL NEED:

Fine and heavy gauge stub wire

Stem tape

Fine reel wire

1 stem Dendrobium orchid (we used John Storei)

1 red rose

1 stem baby's breath

1 stem white spray roses

1 stem pink spray roses

Ivy leaves

Length of ribbon

Join several stub wires together so that they are slightly longer than you want the finished ring to be, and cover them in stem tape. Find the center and wire on the orchids with reel wire, followed by the looped and wired red rose. Then use reel wire to attach the baby's breath and spray roses in turn to each side, along with the ivy leaves. Complete the ring by pulling the two ends together and tying them with ribbon.

ɑPPLE jACK

This foliage ball, decorated with shiny ripe apples, is a lovely idea for harvest time. It would look just right on a scrubbed-pine kitchen table, and it lasts for a long time ~ simply replace the fruit when it begins to wrinkle. Use a similar pattern as for the step-by-step table center to build up a basic framework, then fill in each section.

YOU WILL NEED:

Floral foam and tape

Flat dish or small plate

8–10 sprigs laurel

Spray leaf shine

12 apples

12 sticks or taped stub wires

TIP
Polish the apples with vegetable oil to give them a lovely gloss.

Cut a standard block of floral foam in half, and put one half on top of the other on the dish and tape them together. Add foliage all around, keeping the lengths even. If the foam is visible, fill the gaps with leaves stuck straight into the foam. Turn all around to check the silhouette is even before spraying with leaf shine. Place the apples on sticks or wires (see Lemon Tree on page 28), and arrange them evenly around the foliage ball.

ƒLORAL ƒRUIT ƀOWL

This decorative floral frame makes a real feature of a fruit bowl on the sideboard when you are entertaining at home. The soft froth of the baby's breath is quickly taped in place, and it transforms the bare wires. You can use any color of flowers in the top knot and at the sides to coordinate with your furnishings.

Tape together three stub wires and cover them with stem tape before adding baby's breath and asparagus fern, leaving clear an inch at either end. Repeat three times more, then twist together the four covered bundles at one end. Open up the wires gently in curves and attach to the bowl with fixing putty, spacing them equally. Skewer a small foam block on the joined, twisted ends, and add the hare's foot fern and carnations. Complete with ivy trails and orange safflowers. Add more flowers and foliage to the base of two of the loops, and fill the container with fruit.

The foam will drip water into the bowl, so make the arrangement the day before if water will spoil the contents.

hostess bouquet

This is an ideal way of presenting flowers to a friend because they can be prepared in advance and sit in their own reserve of water. Your hostess simply removes the cellophane wrapper and places the tied arrangement in a vase.

YOU WILL NEED:

1 piece tingiringi gum
1 piece eucalyptus
3 sprigs of heather
3 pieces baby's breath
4 spray carnations
10 roses
Green twine
2 large squares cellophane
Florist's ribbon

Build up the bouquet in your hand in a similar way to the Hand-tie Bouquet (see page 42). Separate the foliage stems into pieces that can be evenly spread through the bouquet. Starting with the foliage, look at the arrangement from above as well as the sides, but keep some in reserve to finish off the outside. Add the key flowers, the roses, at the very last.

You can tie the bouquet as you go along, or you can wait until all the pieces are in place. Tie firmly together before trimming the stems level – the aim is that the bouquet should stand on its stems. Lay the bouquet so that the stem ends are in the center of the cellophane squares, and gather up the excess all around. Add water to the pocket holding the stems before tying tightly and finishing with a florist's bow (see page 24).

tYING A fLORIST'S bOW

A ribbon can make a flower arrangement into a gift in seconds or it can be used to add a seasonal flavor. Florist's ribbon is simple to split into different widths, which means that you can make this bow as big and bold or as delicate as you wish by using the same method and same material. Here's how to tie a bow that works every time and always looks good.

1 Form a loop with the ribbon but keep it flat. Make a twist in what will become the center, then form another loop on the other side, pinch together and twist again.

2 Repeat this figure-eight pattern once more, letting the loops get larger and remembering to pinch the ribbon together before you twist to stop the loops from twisting, too.

3 Continue as before until the bow is as large as you want. Tie a narrow piece of florist's ribbon around the center to hold the bow in shape, then either trim the edges to make the tails or make fake tails by adding a length of ribbon to the center.

tEA tIME

The blue and yellow in the design in this cracked teapot have been used as the palette for the flowers in the posy. This arrangement would make a great feature on a kitchen table, and it makes excellent use of an old teapot.

YOU WILL NEED:

Teapot
Floral foam
1 stem asparagus fern
Bear grass
6 timothy grass (cattails)
9 stems asters
1 stem prairie gentian
9 yellow roses

Wedge the floral foam firmly into the top of the pot so that it stands 2 inches above the rim; shape it into a rough round. Make an initial foliage ball by inserting the fern, bear grass, and cattails all over the foam, then add the longest stems of aster, spacing them evenly. Finally, divide the prairie gentian into separate pieces to place around the ball and add the roses as contrast, leaving rose foliage around the stems to help cover the floral foam. Finish off with rose leaves around the base of the arrangement, too.

WILLOW WREATH

Make a refreshingly different sort of wreath for your door this year by using this dragon's claw willow and moss base. The basic covered ring can be used time and time again ~ you simply replace the floral foam and the fresh flowers when they become exhausted.

YOU WILL NEED:

Bag of sphagnum moss

Metal ring frame

Reel of wire

2 stems dragon's claw willow

4 handfuls colored reindeer moss

Small piece floral foam and floral tape

2 proteas with foliage

2 anthuriums

TIP
All the material except the anthuriums will dry to create a permanent wreath.

Bind the sphagnum moss to the **top** of the frame using the wire until it is evenly covered all over. Cut the fine tips off the willow in about 6-inch lengths, and bind pieces together with the reindeer moss all around the top of the ring using the wire. Attach small bundles at a time, and work your way around to where you started. Tape a small block of floral foam tightly to one point of the ring, then build up the foliage and flowers to create the floral accent.

TALL
ARRANGEMENTS

Some flowers look their best when they
are left with long stems, and some tall
containers somehow never look right,
whatever you try in them. We have looked
at both these problems and come up with
10 really good-looking solutions.
The problem with tall flower stems or
large containers is that the sense of scale
you may find easy on smaller
arrangements – that is, the balance
between the foliage, flowers and container
– becomes altogether much more difficult
to judge. You will find yourself having to
step well back from the arrangement far
more often, and you will need to work on
a table just as you would for smaller
arrangements. Do not be tempted to place
the container on the floor, because the
balance will be much more difficult
to assess.

Making a Tall Arrangement Work

You may have experimented with a favorite vase or tried using elegant, tall flowers on numerous occasions, and yet somehow the result never looks right. This is because your eye tells you that the balance is wrong – there is too much flower at the top or too much vase at the bottom – and that is quite apart from getting the balance of colors and the selection of foliage right.

If you look at many of the tall arrangements in this section, you will see that they use one of the flower arrangers' golden rules: the material in the vase is twice the height of the vase or container. We all know that rules are there to be broken, and this pattern is often abandoned with small arrangements or, as we can see in the case of the white lilies on page 35, when the proportion is half and half; but in general this principle helps these tall arrangements work particularly well.

As with all other types of arrangement, the spaces you leave are as important as the spaces you fill, so do not try to overcrowd the stems of the flowers and foliage you are using just because the whole piece is so much larger than the size you may be used to working in. By using the larger, taller containers, you will also be able to use flowers more dramatically than is possible when you are working on a smaller scale – compare the effect of the gladioli in the three arrangements in which they feature, for example – and you will be able to make the most of the contrast or harmony of the colors you have chosen because there will be so much more of it.

*l*EMON *t*REE

This clever idea of combining fruit and foliage to create a tree is simple, yet effective. The tall tree looks really bright and fresh – it would be perfect for a summer lunch party. It can be viewed from all sides, although you should choose the height of the storage jar carefully because the top block of floral foam can add a lot of weight and make the tree top heavy if the jar is too tall or narrow.

YOU WILL NEED:

25–30 lemons

Tall glass vase

Floral foam and floral tape

10 pieces bay or similar foliage

Spray leaf shine

Stub wire and stem tape

1 Put some lemons in the vase so that they almost reach the top, but leave space for the floral foam. The lemons should fit tightly or they will float when you add the water. Fill the vase with water, then place a floral foam plug on top; you may want to tape it in place. Pare the foam down to a roundish shape before adding a foliage cross.

2 Divide the ball into four quarters and fill in a quarter of the ball at a time, using leaves close to the foam as well as on even length stems so that it is completely covered.

3 Check all around the completed ball that the circle is even, and adjust as necessary. Spray with leaf shine.

4 Bind three stub wires together with stem tape, and fold over one end by about ½ inch to form a hook. Push the wires through the center of the lemons until the hooked end just disappears into the skin of the lemon. You may need to make a pilot hole with a skewer to prevent the tape from being stripped as you pull the wire through.

5 Place the lemons in position, turning the vase around so that they are evenly distributed.

SINGLY SIMPLE

These regal stems of white lilies maintain their freshness in the clear glass vase and marbles, which hide the stems. This dramatic arrangement would be just as at home in a simple, almost plain room as in one filled with rich colors and drapes, for both would offer complementary foils to these delicate trumpets.

YOU WILL NEED:

Tall glass vase

3–4 containers clear glass marbles

10 stems single and multi-head white trumpet lilies

TIP
Using marbles to support flowers is an effective way of using a glass vase because they disguise the sometimes unattractive stems.

Fill the vase three-quarters with marbles, then fill it with water.

Remove the lower leaves from the stems of the lilies and add them to the vase, one at a time, pushing them into the marbles and turning the trumpets to the right direction as you do so. Place shorter stems near the front. Once all the stems are in place, trim off any excess foliage above the rim of the vase, which may make it look too tight – a few leaves from each stem should be enough. Lilies like these spend most of their lives in bud, so if you want a grand show buy them before you need them so that they have time to open slowly.

WIRING A flower

1 ... **2** ... **3**

Some flowers arrive with drooping heads, while others need help to support their heavy heads in an arrangement. You may want to control the direction in which the flowers face. Whatever the reason, knowing how to wire a flower can save many arrangements.

1 Using a piece of stub wire, insert the tip into the stem of the flower just behind the sepals and far enough to hold firm.

2 Gently twist the wire around the stem of the flower, moving down in a spiral. If your arrangement is not going to be closely examined, you can stop now.

3 To hide the wire, cover it with stem tape, starting at the top by the flower head and twisting the stem as you guide the tape into position over the wire.

CHINA blue

This dramatic vase could easily overpower the delphiniums if they were used on their own. The willow and white flowers not only tie in with the colors of the dragon design on the vase itself, but also help to balance the strength of the design with dramatic action above. Place the arrangement in a colorless corner in a hall or landing.

YOU WILL NEED:

Large vase, preferably blue and white

5 pieces dragon's claw willow

5 stems delphiniums

10 stars-of-Bethlehem

7 long stems eucalyptus

TIP
Use long-stemmed flowers and foliage, which will bend and curve to add width to an otherwise rigid composition.

Put about 5 inches of water in the bottom of the vase. Position the willow stems so that they create an overall shape; use both thick and wispy end pieces. Then add the delphinium stems, cutting only a small amount from each so that they all stand at different heights and so that the longest is about 3 inches shorter than the tallest piece of willow. Add the stars-of-Bethlehem (you could use long-stemmed carnations). Trim the eucalyptus so that you use single long stems with only one or two side shoots, and position them throughout the vase.

*P*EACE *T*IME

Arrangements such as this, which use one type of flower and one predominant color, can be truly effective. There are, in fact, three colors in this selection of flowers – soft white, green, and yellow – and three types of stem. Even the vase is a soft white so that the whole effect is of glowing freshness and innocence, which ideally suits the arum lilies.

YOU WILL NEED:

Vase

10 pieces variegated euonymus

2 pieces wild mignonette

9 arum lilies

TIP
Slit the stems of the lilies to permit maximum water take-up, and change the water every two to three days.

Fill the vase with water, then add long lengths of euonymus to provide both an outline shape and support for the lily stems. Add the wild mignonette evenly, keeping the pieces long at the back and shorter towards the front. Cut the lily stems to different heights, and space them around the vase.

ＳUNNY ＤAY

Sunflowers towering in the garden look so regal, but it is often difficult to make them look impressive once you have cut them and brought them inside. This bright, showy arrangement makes the most of the glossy, green vase, which suits the flowers perfectly, and it would be an ideal way of adding color to a summer fireplace or dark hall corner.

YOU WILL NEED:

Large plain vase

Large floral foam blocks to fit and fill the container, extending approximately 3 inches above the rim

3 large sunflowers

1 stem laurel

5 stems throatwort

7 long-stemmed alliums

9 stalks graminae (ken grass)

Push the foam blocks firmly into the vase, and position the three sunflowers at different heights in the center of the container. Add the laurel around the base of the vase and to the front, covering the join between the floral foam and the vase. Position the throatwort evenly around, maintaining the length, the alliums and the ken grass, remembering to place the stems behind, at the sides and at the front of the arrangement.

> **TIP**
> If sunflower heads are too heavy for the stems, try wiring them; see page 32.

10-inch plastic bowl

3 blocks floral foam and floral tape

3 sprigs each variegated euonymus, brown, glycerined beech, and eucalyptus

5 stems white gladioli

5 stems tiger lilies

12 white carnations

3 stems orange euphorbia

Arrange the foam in the bowl, with two blocks in the bottom and a central block sitting 3 inches above the rim, and tape them securely in place. Make a tall, wide triangle with the euonymus, remembering to put some at the front of the bowl, too. Add beech, mainly around the base of the bowl, and eucalyptus to echo the euonymus. Arrange the gladioli stems in a line down the center, with two coming forwards from the base. Add the lilies at the base, in a gentle curve from right to left rather than in a straight line, and the carnations in a taller curve from left to right. Finally, strip the leaves from the euphorbia and add the stems to the bottom right of the arrangement.

*p*YRAMID *r*HYTHM

This dramatic swathe of orange and white would be as appropriate in a niche or alcove as stood on a dramatic pillar in an entrance hall – wherever it is, it is bound to make an impression. Simply change the color of the lilies and use snowberry instead of euphorbia if you want to match your color scheme.

> **TIP**
> Always wash your hands after handling euphorbia because the creamy sap is an irritant if it gets into your eyes.

*O*LD-TIME *E*LEGANCE

This arrangement in a pitcher or bowl, with its showers of bear grass and fresh irises, would make a refreshing addition to a bedroom or bathroom.

TIP
Take care when you handle bear grass because the leaf edges are razor sharp.

YOU WILL NEED:

Large pitcher or vase

Floral foam to fill container

1 trailing ivy plant

10 lilac liatris

11 blue or purple irises

Approximately 24 stalks bear grass

Stub wire

Fill the container with foam. Separate the ivy into clumps, and position them so that they trail out of the spout and over the sides. Fan out the liatris and irises, and use iris foliage to fill the shape around the sides and back. Bunch bear grass in groups of four or five stems with stub wires, and insert the bunches around the front and middle of the pitcher.

MAY POLE

A tall moss pole, flanking the church door or placed in the porch, would be a fitting decoration for a country wedding. The china asters are like bright jewels, and they can be replaced when necessary with new blooms if you continue to mist the moss itself; alternatively, the entire arrangement may be left to dry.

YOU WILL NEED:

Wooden bucket or large plant pot

Moss pole

Cement or plaster of paris to secure pole

2 bags additional sphagnum moss

Reel of wire

Stub wire

14 stems china asters

1 piece heather

Line the container with plastic if you wish to reuse it, and set the pole in concrete. Starting at the bottom, wire an additional layer of moss to the pole, using the reel wire and working your way up the pole. Lay out a sausage-shape of extra moss to make the spiralling swag and wire this together with reel wire. Attach the spiral to the pole, again using reel wire to hold it in place. Cut the heads off the china asters and pin them to the spiral in groups of three, using folded pins of stub wire. Add two sprigs of heather to each cluster.

exotic highlight

This striking arrangement makes the most of these dark spears of gladioli, mixing reds, yellows, and oranges to create a bright,

YOU WILL NEED:

Bucket or tub container, plus plastic liner if needed
Floral foam
10 stems red gladioli
6 lilies (4 orange, 2 yellow)
4 large strelitzia leaves
Blue and natural reindeer moss to cover floral foam
Stub wires or German pins

Line the pot, if necessary, and insert the foam blocks. Position the long gladioli stems first, placing them in a group towards the back of the container. Add long stems of orange lilies, with shorter yellow lilies to one side, in front of the gladioli. Finish off with the large leaves, positioning them to frame the base. Cover the floral foam with moss, using wires or pins to hold it securely.

TIP
Any large leaves will do for this arrangement — large banana leaves are just as effective. Spray them with leaf shine to give extra gloss.

CHOCOLATE CENTER

This is an original idea for offering chocolates or treats to your guests. The salmon-pink and purple make a fine combination, but you could very easily give the whole thing a festive flavor by using red and white flowers – use red roses instead of prairie gentians, and white gerbera and gladioli instead of pink blooms.

YOU WILL NEED:

Cakestand or similar pedestal container
Floral foam and tape
1 stem eucalyptus
5 stems pink gladioli
6 stems salmon-pink gerbera
2 stems prairie gentians
Florist's ribbon
Silver-covered paper cake board

TIP
If you use a plastic pedestal and fix it to the board with floral putty, this arrangement can be wrapped in cellophane and given as a gift.

Tape the floral foam to the cake-stand and make an outline with a tall triangle of eucalyptus. Use the gladioli tops to accentuate the shape, and use the trimmed ends of the shorter spears to fill in the sides. Keeping the gerbera towards the center, cut the stems down, using the extra lengths to add to the framework of foliage.

Break up the prairie gentians, and place the tall lengths towards the back and the unopened buds so that they droop to the front. Add a small florist's bow in co-ordinating ribbon to the center of the arrangement (see page 24), place the arrangement on a ribbon-edged board, and add the chocolates.

SYMMETRICAL ARRANGEMENTS

The opportunities for using a symmetrical arrangement in the home are numerous –
on a mantelpiece, dressing table or hall table, or as a table centerpiece, for example –
and the results are pleasing to the eye. However, much has been written and said
about the skills required to produce a symmetrical arrangement, and this has tended
to make them one of the most avoided patterns.

True symmetry is a form that the eye does not always find interesting,
because there may be no focal point on which it can settle. In many of these
arrangements, therefore, you will notice that although the shape and basic
form of the arrangement are completely symmetrical, there is an addition of
central color, which may upset the carefully established symmetry, like
the liatris in Bateau Bleu (page 53). Alternatively, the entire arrangement
may be symmetrical only in basic form, as in the Dramatic Dahlias (page 46).

Making a Symmetrical Arrangement

To create a symmetrical arrangement you need to imagine vertical and horizontal lines drawn through the center of the container you are planning to use. For true symmetry, the foliage and flowers on each side of the vertical line should be a mirror image. However, although the two sides of the arrangement should appear the same, they do not have to be identical, although the balance of color and shape should be basically the same, and the outline shape should be symmetrical. You will notice that the basic shape of many of these arrangements is the triangle, with the tall, central piece of foliage becoming the central vertical line to help to keep the arrangement in shape. The larger flowers have been used to add shape and curves to the arrangement without disturbing the outline shape and balance of the foliage.

We have chosen a wide variety of containers and flowers to show how basic symmetry can be used to enhance both the shape of the container as well as the properties of the blooms and foliage. The step-by-step Hand-tie Bouquet, in particular, is a method we think you will find very useful because it is a good way of keeping your arrangement in shape without the use of floral foam or other materials.

A *h*AND-TIE *b*OUQUET

This is a symmetrical arrangement in outline only. The simplest way to build up this bouquet is to look at the whole arrangement in the mirror at each stage so that you can check

YOU WILL NEED:

4 sprigs heather
1 sprig wild mignonette
12 stems eucalyptus
Garden twine
2 bunches love-in-a-mist
1 bunch bear grass
4 stems Aster ericoides
3 stems milkweed
3 deep pink asters
4 pink spray roses

for color balance and positioning. There is no need for the flowers and foliage to be in total symmetry, as this example shows, and you may well decide to make the arrangement more symmetrical in color than this. The overall effect is created by the variety, not the quantity, of stems used.

1 Separate the heather, wild mignonette, and eucalyptus into pieces, and arrange the heather with eight of the longer pieces of eucalyptus in your hand. Add the mignonette evenly, and bind loosely.

2 Add the longest stems of love-in-a-mist in pairs to the center of the bundle, along with groups of bear grass all around the outside. Bind again with the twine.

3 Squeeze the stems of *Aster ericoides* into the center. Begin checking the shape regularly in a large mirror, and keep repositioning the stems until you are happy with the shape. Bind again.

4 Add the milkweed and asters to the center. Add more shorter foliage around the outside.

5 Add the key flowers last, in this case the roses, so that they are visible from the front. Add any additional foliage and smaller pieces of love-in-a-mist to the outside of the bunch, then bind to hold. Trim off the stems evenly.

♪UMMER ♪YMPHONY

This wonderful collection of fragrant freesias and dark anemones would make a lovely centerpiece for a celebration. The delicate oak pedestal adds the height needed to show this arrangement off to best advantage, although you may like to position it instead on either a mantelpiece or shelf.

YOU WILL NEED:

U-shaped plain vase
Floral foam, wire, and tape
2 coordinating colored candles
2 stems of Aster ericoides
6 trails ivy
10 long-stemmed pink freesias
10 long-stemmed lilac freesias
4 purple anemones
8 pink anemones
2 white anemones

TIP
The whole arrangement has been ringed by intertwined green ivy and butcher's broom to add to the effect.

Position a piece of floral foam in the neck of the vase so that it fits tightly and protrudes 3 inches above the rim; tape it in position. Position the candles in the center; you can either tape folded stub wire to the bases to form prongs to pin them to the floral foam, or use candle handlers. Make an initial crescent (called Hogarth's line) using the asters, then add the ivy trails to the outside corners.

Use the long-stemmed freesias to echo the curved outline you have made, and leave the central portion of the space for the anemones. Position anemones in the center, keeping some in reserve to cover the base. Fix floral foam to the base of the vase and press in ivy, asters, and short stems of anemone to cover.

DRAMATIC DAHLIAS

This up-turned, crescent-shaped arrangement makes the most of home-grown dahlias, and is perfect for their heavy, velvety heads. The plain vase and cream tuberoses lighten what could otherwise be too heavy, and the finished result is a really rich concoction.

YOU WILL NEED:

Vase

Floral foam

1 sprig of brown, glycerined beech

12 dark red dahlias

2 stems tuberose, broken into heads

3 deep purple snapdragons

TIP
This arrangement makes the most of the dark shades of the flowers, but you could use lighter blooms if you wanted to make an arrangement to brighten a dark corner.

Wedge the floral foam into the vase, with the top extending about 2 inches above the rim. Arrange the beech foliage in a soft curve, with the longest stems at the sides. Then add the dahlias, including the evenly distributed buds and foliage, dividing the vase in half down the vertical center to maintain a symmetrical balance. The white tuberoses are placed in a subtle diagonal line to the center, while the three snapdragons are in a line down the center.

REGAL SPREAD

Perfect for festive decoration, this wide arrangement, with hot-house carnations and roses, can be recreated on even the coldest winter day. Although we have designed it for a side table or mantelpiece, it could very easily be adapted for a wedding centerpiece.

YOU WILL NEED:

Flat, rectangular dish
Floral foam and tape
Candle
5 stems sugar pine
10 red spray carnations
5 large red carnations
5 white roses
2 white spray roses
2 pieces snowberry
2 trails jasmine

TIP
Check that the sugar pine is fresh by pulling it through your hand and watching for falling needles.

Secure the floral foam in the dish with tape, and position the candle in the center. Make a wide, flat triangle with the sugar pine, using both sides of the foliage to vary the color, and placing short lengths around the candle. Add the flowers symmetrically and evenly all over, checking for balance of color and variety in length so that the flower heads can be seen. Finish off with the snowberry and trails of jasmine towards the front.

CARING for Cut roses

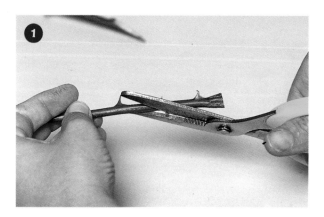

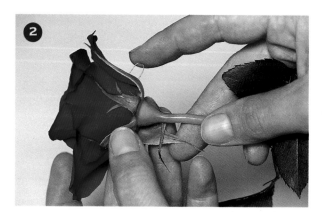

Roses bought from your florist can often be expensive, and if you are lucky enough to receive them you will want them to look their best for as long as possible.

1 Once you are ready to use the stems, strip off the lower leaves and recut the stems to length with a long, angular cut to provide the maximum surface area for a water intake.

2 If you want your roses to stay in bud, make small, U-shaped pins out of short lengths of silver wire. Fold up the sepal around the petals and hold it in position by pushing the pin into the heart of the rose. Repeat this for all the sepals on the rose and then use the rose as normal.

> **TIP**
> You can tell how fresh the roses at the florist are by looking at the color of the cut end of the stem — it should be the same bright green as the stem. Look out for tell-tale, dark brown rings, which tell you that the flowers have already been in the shop a few days.

CLASSIC CONTRAST

This composition is a good example of an almost perfect symmetrical arrangement, with just one of the yellow lilies being slightly off-center. This arrangement is ideal for a hall table because it is so compact.

YOU WILL NEED:

Pedestal container
Floral foam and tape
3 stems variegated euonymus
4 dark gladioli
3 snapdragons, the same color as the gladioli
2 yellow lilies

Secure the foam in position on the pedestal. Form a low triangle with the euonymus before placing the gladioli tips symmetrically at the back to add height to the triangle. Use the short lengths cut from the gladioli spears to add to the outline shape. Add gladioli foliage at the back to fill in, then add the snapdragons. Use shorter lengths of euonymus to hide the floral foam, and finally position two large, open lilies in the center.

*b*RIGHT *ſ*TAR

This star-shaped table center-piece is ideal for a large, low coffee table, which will allow your skills to be fully appreciated. The refreshing combination of yellow and green makes it perfect for brightening up the room, and it could easily be the only arrangement you need.

YOU WILL NEED:

Flat, rectangular dish

Floral foam and tape

1 piece variegated euonymus

1 stem eucalyptus

3 white spray roses

8 stems veronica

4 stems white euphorbia

2 yellow lilies

4 yellow alstroemerias

TIP

When you make compositions like this, it helps if you can work on a lower surface so that you can view the design from overhead as you build it up.

Tape floral foam in place on the dish, then use the euonymus to make an initial star shape. Add some cover in the center, before adding eucalyptus to the points of the star and the center. Position the roses, veronica, and euphorbia at the four points, with the lilies and remaining veronica towards the center. Add the alstroemerias to the center of the star, varying their lengths so that they extend to the points. Keep turning the dish to make sure that the design is even on both sides, and match every stem you position with another in the other three corresponding points of the star.

ƒOLIAGE tREE

What a simple idea, yet so easy to make and so effective! This foliage tree can feature any color of flower you wish, but there is nothing so crisp as the combination of yellow and deep, glossy green. The result is perfect for a sideboard or kitchen table, and the flowers can be replaced time and time again while the foliage remains fresh.

YOU WILL NEED:

Plant pot

Plastic sheet for lining

Floral foam

4 pieces bay or laurel

Spray leaf shine

5 spray chrysanthemums

Stub wires

TIP
When you have completed the peak of the tree, wire or tie the foliage out of the way so that you can add the lower branches more easily.

Wedge a piece of foam upright in a lined plant pot so that it sits about 5 inches above the rim. Trim the top to a rounded point. Starting at the top of the foam, gradually add longer pieces of foliage to make a tree effect, turning the pot all the time and letting the pieces get gradually longer as you work downwards. Check the shape and make sure you have covered all the foam before spraying with leaf shine. Taking each chrysanthemum head in turn, insert a stub wire and position it in a spiral on the tree, starting at the top and working your way around and down.

t ASTIE m AISIE

TIP
Keep the flowers in color groups for the greatest effect.

Florists often sell pre-packed mixed bouquets that, on first examination, seem to offer very little in the way of color co-ordination and style. Here, with the addition of just a few pieces of foliage, four mixed bouquets have been combined to make a dramatic presentation basket. The smaller the basket, the fewer flowers you will need, of course.

YOU WILL NEED:

Small, deep, plastic-lined basket

Floral foam and tape

1 sprig sugar pine

1 sprig eucalyptus

2 sprigs butcher's broom

1 stem brown, glycerined beech

12 mixed chrysanthemum stems
(4 one color, 8 a different color)

2 spray carnations

4 carnations

2 lilies

Secure the floral foam in the basket so that it extends about 3 inches above the top edge. Form the basic triangle all round with the sugar pine and fill in with eucalyptus, with the butcher's broom falling to the front. Place the beech in the key points of the triangle: center back, sides, and center front. Add the chrysanthemums evenly throughout, then introduce the spray carnations, keeping the central area for the larger key flowers, in this case the single carnations and the lilies.

*b*ATEAU *b*LEU

The boat-shaped table arrangement is one of the classic symmetrical arrangements. Once you have mastered this composition, you will be able to use it time and time again. Simply change the colored stems for equal quantities of similarly shaped flowers to re-create your own color scheme.

YOU WILL NEED:

Small rectangular or oval dish

Floral foam and tape

1 stem sugar pine

2 stems heather

12 spray carnations

12 single carnations

6 stems chrysanthemums

10 stems liatris

Tape the floral foam securely to the dish. Make an outline using sugar pine, with two long points at the shorter sides of the rectangle and two shorter points at the centers of the longer sides. Arrange the sugar pine so that it curves between these two points. Add foliage to the top to make the shape three-dimensional, before filling in evenly with the heather, carnations, and chrysanthemums. The liatris is used to provide interest on the two sides by creating an additional diagonal line.

Sweet Perfection

This is a lovely, low arrangement for a hall or a bedroom, and the thistles open up into pretty pompoms in the warm air indoors.

TIP
Use buds of *Aster ericoides* rather than open flowers to contribute to the soft green background.

YOU WILL NEED:

Small bowl

Floral foam and tape

5 stems Aster ericoides

5 stems protea foliage (or any fresh green foliage)

12 pieces asparagus fern

1 stem baby's breath

20 centaurea thistles

10 irises

Tape the floral foam into the bowl so that it sits about 2 inches above the rim. Make an initial fan shape across the back with the asters, then continue by filling in around the front. Use the five lime green pieces of protea at the front, then fill in, using the fern and baby's breath. Distribute the thistle evenly over the shape before adding the irises in the spaces.

Asymmetrical
Arrangements

While creating a symmetrical arrangement can be difficult, making the most of asymmetrical patterns in flower arrangements can be seen as too daring for the home. They are, however, well worth the effort, because there will be many occasions when you do not need a centrally placed display of flowers or when an asymmetrical design can be offset by other ornaments or items – in fact, these can be used to guide your color choice and container size.

Arrangements in which the balance of the flowers and foliage is uneven can be very effective, and we have come up with some simple ideas for you to try yourself. Once you have seen how the style can be used, we hope you will be more adventurous with your own ideas.

An awareness of the weight that different colors of flowers or foliage give to an arrangement is a great help when you are tackling the asymmetrical shape, and you will notice that the focal point of many of these examples is still central, with only the outline shape being set asymmetrically to the imaginary vertical line we use in symmetrical arrangements. If it helps, lay a pencil grid over the pictures for the vertical and horizontal balance to help analyze the shapes for yourself.

Making an Asymmetrical Arrangement

The starting point of many of these arrangements is a perfectly ordinary vase or pot, and you can see how the shape has been built up in just the same way as for the round and symmetrical styles before. However, instead of concentrating on matching, the balance is now set askew to the imaginary square grid used to guide us before. The trick is to keep the visual balance of color and size between the two sides the same, but to change the shape so that the eye is drawn in a different direction, from one side to the other. You will see that the flowers are often in more symmetry than in the sym-metrical arrangements, but with the addition of extra length to one corner or with large, key blooms used to take the eye off the central area.

In some cases, of course, the container lends itself to an asymmetrical balance – a gravy boat or pitcher, for example, will allow you to emphasize the shape by extending the flowers and foliage along the curves of the container.

We are sure that once you have reproduced these stunning arrangements yourself, you will find the asymmetrical style one of the easiest to create with panache.

A Simple Corsage

Use this delicate-looking corsage to decorate your dress or hand-bag for a formal dinner or dance, and it will be much admired. The five, tape-covered silver wires hold the stems in the per-fect position so that you can control the overall shape.

YOU WILL NEED:
5 stems freesias
Fine silver wire
Stem tape
1 long stub wire for the spine
1 small piece ivy
1 small piece baby's breath
1 small piece heather

1 Break the freesia stems into individual large flowers and groups of buds, leaving the small pieces of stem attached to hold the flower together. Pierce the flower above the sepal with a piece of silver wire.

2 Fold down the wire, leaving one end longer than the other to create a long stem, then twist the long wire over the short piece of flower stem and the other shorter wire to make a firm join.

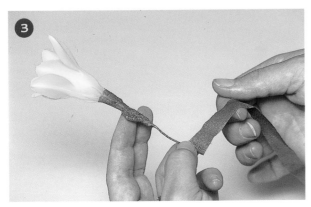

3 Starting at the flower head, cover the wire in stem tape by twisting the tape over the wires. Repeat with all the pieces of freesia, adding the long stub wire spine to a set of closed buds, which will form the point in the finished corsage.

4 Wire up individual ivy leaves of all sizes by spearing the back main vein in the leaf with a silver wire before folding it down and taping it in the same way as you prepared the flower heads.

5 After grouping all your ingredients by size, collect together a small posy. Start with the freesia buds on the long stub wire, add in some short heather stems and small ivy leaves, and then tape them together to form the top of the corsage. Gradually add larger flowers and ivy leaves, bending the wire stems out to widen the shape. Open out the corsage in the center before using small pieces again at the bottom, leaving a short length of the stub wire to curl around at the end. Add small pieces of baby's breath to the center to soften the overall shape.

TIP
The block of floral foam must be absolutely firm before you start. If you use rosemary or a similarly fragrant foliage in a candle arrangement, the warmth of the flame will help to release the perfume.

*W*HITE *L*IGHT

Stand this on your mantelpiece or make the arrangement to fit a newel post and bring a touch of delicate summer color into your home. It would be perfect for a wedding or christening celebration at home, with the spears of bear grass softening the whole shape.

YOU WILL NEED:

Floral foam, about 2 inches square, frog, fixing putty, and tape
Candlestick and candle
12–15 pieces bear grass
5 trails ivy
7 pieces butcher's broom
6 pieces rosemary
1 stem mauve alstroemeria
10 stems white sweet pea
Small length florist's ribbon and wire

Fix the floral foam to the candlestick using a frog and fixing putty, then tape it securely all around the back. Make the outline shape, which is a skewed oval, with the bear grass and ivy, placing a trail on the bottom left-hand side to drop the shape slightly. Complete the overall shape with butcher's broom and rosemary. Add heads of alstroemeria in a band of color across the center, with the stems longer on the left than the right to bring the shape down towards the ivy. Finally, position the sweet peas in two bands either side of the alstroemeria, with one longer stem extending on the left. Add bow tails in florist's ribbon.

*t*HREE IN *O*NE

This patriotic display of red and white on blue uses three clay flowerpots salvaged from the garden shed to add a rustic touch to a glossy arrangement, which could otherwise look overpolished.

YOU WILL NEED:

3 clay flowerpots of different sizes
Polythene or plastic to line the pots
Floral foam
6 arum lilies
stub wire
8 anthuriums
9 stems hare's foot fern
9 stalks bear grass, wired in clusters
8 pieces dragon's claw willow

Line the pots, then trim the floral foam so that it almost fits to the top of each pot; press it in. Make holes in the foam to accommodate the thick stems of the arum lilies, and then place two lilies in each pot. Add off-cuts of stems to give more height and shape to the composition. Position the anthuriums before framing the flowers with pieces of fern, bear grass, and dragon's claw willow.

> **TIP**
> Always line clay or terracotta pots because water from the floral foam will drip through.

GOLDEN CHEER

Deep golden-yellow with green and just a touch of mauve make this striking asymmetrical arrangement a bold statement to have on a side table or dressing table. The plain jello mold is an ideal foil, because the shapes of the flowers and foliage provide plenty of interest.

YOU WILL NEED:

Jello mold or similar wide-necked container
Floral foam
5 stems box
3 sprigs heather
3 pieces wild mignonette
20 craspedias
2 stems orange euphorbia

Create the outline triangular shape with box and heather, making the front bottom right corner lower than the other. Cut the lengths of mignonette slightly shorter, then add them to echo this shape. Arrange the craspedias in a similar shape. Add the euphorbia last, filling in any gaps with short pieces of box and heather.

> **TIP**
> Euphorbia is very seasonal. Use pyracantha blossom or berries to give a similar frothy effect if you cannot find any stems of euphorbia.

PITCHER PERFECT

This dark, moody collection of deep reds, mauves, and blues would be perfect on a dining table or sideboard.

YOU WILL NEED:

Gravy boat or similar low pitcher

Floral foam

15 red, purple, and deep pink anemones

10 cornflowers

3 sprigs heather

Wedge floral foam firmly into the container so that it stands proud of the rim by 2 inches. Position anemones and cornflowers so that the larger flowers are on the top and the smaller flowers at the sides. Keep the stems very short so that they do not droop (you may need to wire the anemones if the stems are too soft to push into the foam; see page 32). Finally, fill in with small pieces of heather.

CELEBRATION SWAG

Once you have perfected this very simple swag there will be no end to the occasions when you can adapt it ~ christenings, weddings, birthdays, or Christmas. Any time you need to dress up a doorway, mantelpiece or table, this swag can be quickly put together in a color scheme to match your furnishings.

YOU WILL NEED:

4 pieces of butcher's broom

Stub wire

2 stems baby's breath

14 spider chrysanthemums

First wire the lengths of butcher's broom together, overlapping the growing end with the next cut end so that it has an even shape. Wire clusters of baby's breath to individual spider flowers, then space them evenly along the length of the butcher's broom swag. When you have finished, give the whole swag a refreshing spray and continue to do so regularly to keep the flowers fresh.

These materials will make a swag about 4 feet long; simply multiply the materials by the number of lengths you need.

CLEAR JEWEL

The rich, deep, velvety jewel colors of these anemones make a perfect triangle of color, with just the liatris and the foliage taking the eye off to the right to create the asymmetry. This elegant display is perfect for a shelf or side table.

YOU WILL NEED:

Glass vase
Clay pebbles
Floral foam
1 stem tingiringi gum
1 stem butcher's broom
15 anemones
Stub wire
5 stems liatris

Put pebbles in the vase until they are about 2 inches from the top. Push a small block of floral foam into top so that it extends above edge of vase by about 2½ inches. Make the initial outline with the tingiringi gum, then add butcher's broom for more depth. Wire the anemones so that they will push into the floral foam, and position them so that there is a gradual reduction in height in the center. Fill either side, with the longer stems to the left following the line of the foliage. Add liatris to define the shape and add contrast.

Centrepiece

golden wheat-hued linens grace the table, setting off the white china to perfection. Grape twigs peek from place cards, stones from the vineyard secure handwritten menus and tags attached to wine glasses help guests keep track of each wine they sample.

CENTREPIECE

A harvest basket, created by floral desi[...] Rosemary Little of Quince Flower[...] surprisingly easy to make. First, f[...] natural wicker basket that suits the s[...] your table. Line basket with plastic to mai[...] leak-proof. Set 3 or 4 drinking glasses[...] cups inside and cut oasis to fit the interior[...] each glass. Soak oasis with water.

To build the centrepiece, Little chose[...] roses, small purple astrantia, pears, long-stemmed artichokes, bunches of grapes and[...] leafy grapevine, which can be ordered from a[...] florist. Place roses and astrantia in the damp[...] oasis, along with the grapevine. Cluster[...] artichokes and grapes around the flowers to[...] hide the glasses below. Assemble a group of[...] pears by sticking them together with wooden[...] toothpicks or skewers. To finish, weave[...] grapevine gently through the arrangement.

Angelo Pavan

Place Cards

COMBINING THESE SEASONAL, NATURAL ELEMENTS WITH THE PERSONAL TOUCH OF YOUR OWN HANDWRITING HELPS SET A CASUAL, RELAXED TABLE FOR YOUR GUESTS WHILE ALSO PROVIDING INFORMATION FOR THE WINE TASTING.

Signal the end of a long hot summer and welcome autumn in all its rich glory by hosting an outdoor wine country feast. Along with fabulous food, there are some fine Ontario wines for you to discover. Together, through laughter and spirited discussion, you'll learn how different wines complement different foods.

In this season of plenty, a basket brimming with fruits and vegetables makes a fitting centrepiece. Vivid plum and

PLACE CARDS

To continue the natural theme, Nik Manojlovich, host of Savoir Faire, chose exquisite straw-fibre paper from The Japanese Paper Place (887 Queen St. W., Toronto) to create luxurious-looking place cards, menus and wine-tasting booklets. An[...] heavyweight paper, even construction pape[...] would also do the job, says Manojlovich.

Crisp Skinned Salmon
~
Squash Soup with
Chanterelles

Vineland Estates
Winery ~ 1997
Dry Riesling

Inniskillin
1998 Chardonnay

SET THE MOOD FOR A WINE CO

TASTING IN YOUR OWN HOME

DECOR BY NIK MANOJLOVICH   TEXT BY CYNTHIA DAVID   PHOTO

COPPER
CONCOCTION

The bright metal container is a perfect companion to the safflowers used in this arrangement. Combined with the brown, glycerined beech, the russet bulrushes, and the deep colors of the throatwort and gentians, this asymmetrical display is perfect for a hall table in early autumn.

YOU WILL NEED:

Brass pot
Floral foam and tape
2 stems brown, glycerined beech
1 stem eucalyptus
3 bulrushes
10 safflowers
1 stem throatwort
5 stems gentian

Secure the floral foam in the pot so that it stands 2 inches above the rim. Make an asymmetrical outline, using the beech for the main points of the triangle. Add the eucalyptus and bulrushes, then the safflowers to fill in. Use the throatwort to make a focal point at the center and the gentians to add color higher at the back.

EXOTIC STEW

Most of the foliage in this pot came with the large protea flowers, but you could easily use white heather and wild mignonette instead, although this would reduce the overall exotic flavor of the ingredients.

YOU WILL NEED:

Low clay baking pot or similar
Floral foam
5 stems mimosa
1 stem asparagus fern
3 stems protea with foliage
5 stems greater bamboo

Force the foam into the top of the pot so that it sits with about 2 inches above the rim. Use the mimosa and fern to make an initial shape, then add the protea with all the foliage to the central area of the pot, placing a length off to one side. Finish off by using the bamboo to accentuate the shape you have created.

MOSSY MEDLEY

This moss-based wreath would be a colorful welcome into your home if it were placed on a hall table. It takes time and care to build up such a controlled arrangement of color, but the result is really eye-catching.

YOU WILL NEED:

Sphagnum moss ring base
German pins
20 handfuls green bun moss
5 handfuls white lichen moss
10 handfuls red lichen moss
2 handfuls copper-colored lichen moss
Stub wire
5 stems white chrysanthemums
3 stems light green chrysanthemums
Floral foam and tape
1 sprig rosemary
1 sprig heather
1 handful blue reindeer moss
3 stems Aranthera orchids (we used James Storei)

Cover the plain moss ring with bun moss, using the German pins to hold it in place. Add the border bands of colored moss inside and outside, using the same method, and the bands of copper-colored moss across the top. Using the stub wires, pin the chrysanthemum heads to the wreath, using heads that are as similar in size as possible. Stick a band of foam tape around a small block of floral foam, then pin the block to the wreath using stub wires; bridge the tape so that the pin does not pull all the way through the foam. Use the rosemary, heather, and blue reindeer moss to hide the block before you add the orchids.

AWKWARD SHAPES
AND
DIFFICULT FLOWERS

We have all started an arrangement in a new shape of container, only to give up in despair and turn to an old favorite we know how to use, or we have left some exotic blooms languishing in a less than perfect setting – and all for the lack of new ideas. Here we hope to dispel those fears and to show you some more creative solutions to the problems that face everyone from time to time.

A wide variety of exotic flowers and foliage is available from florists, and you will have seen some of it used in projects earlier in the book. Whether it be their scale, shape or color, these tropical plants always look wonderful in the florists, but they can be awkward to deal with once you get them home. Equally, a gift of a container for flowers is always welcome, but sometimes it can take many attempts before you achieve the correct balance of shape and scale. Working with some of the skills you have already developed in the previous sections, these arrangements use a whole range of shapes, styles, and scales to suit the containers or the stems.

USING A
NARROW-NECKED VASE

When you have a vase such as this you often end up relying on the flowers to provide width on their own, which leaves little room in the neck of the vase for foliage or contrast. A block of floral foam instantly makes this vase a glorious show piece. The lilies at the focal point are so perfect that they look like silk.

YOU WILL NEED:

Narrow-necked vase

Floral foam, frog, and fixing putty

---

5 pieces eucalyptus

Bear grass

---

10 long stalks timothy grass (cattails)

---

2 stems heather

---

5 single white roses

---

1 stem white lilies

---

1 Place a ring of fixing putty around the inside of the vase neck to support and secure the frog. Push on and shape a piece of floral foam into a 3-inch round block. Tape. Use pieces of eucalyptus to form the basic symmetrical triangular shape, and add bear grass in threes to fill in the spaces.

2 Use timothy grass to reinforce the triangular outline, and add some of the heather tips to the central area.

3 Continue to add heather tips to the center of the arrangement, then use the roses to add to the central spire and to the outside corners of the now well-defined triangle of foliage.

4 Remove the stamens from two open lilies to prevent the pollen from staining the white petals, then position them at the center, adding closed buds to frame. Fill in any gaps with short stems of heather and eucalyptus to hide the floral foam.

REVIVING flowers IN boILING WATER

Practiced by flower arrangers the world over, this method of reviving flowers and foliage may sound extreme, but it really works. The principle is that the hot water is forced up the stems of the plant, pushing out any air bubbles that may be blocking the passage of water. The method is particularly good for any flowers that have a tendency to drop their heads ~ dahlias, hellebores, fuchsias and anemones, for example. The boiling water treatment can also be used to encourage woody-stemmed flowers, like the roses shown here.

1 Trim an inch or so off the stems, then hold the bottom inch of the stems in boiling water for about 30 seconds, keeping the heads and foliage out of the steam.

You may need to wrap them to prevent damage.

2 Plunge the base of the stems into ice cold water. Hold for about 30 seconds again.

3 Steep the revived stems in a few inches of tepid water for about an hour before use.

bOLD bASKET

The problem of a container that is not waterproof or that has too wide a shape to control the flower stems properly can be overcome by using floral foam in an empty jam jar, as we did in this attractive basket. The combination of foliages with just five stems of yellow lilies is fresh and simple.

YOU WILL NEED:

Unlined basket
Large jam jar to fit basket
Floral foam and putty
1 stem eucalyptus
1 stem bay
5 stems lilies
5 stems greater bamboo

Push the floral foam into the jam jar, then fix the jam jar in the basket with putty. The foam should stand about 2 inches above the rim of the jar, but not above the rim of the basket. Make a wide outline with the eucalyptus and bay. Strip all the foliage from the lilies before you add them, placing them at a variety of heights to support the shape you have created. Add the bamboo and use them to fill around the whole arrangement.

tROPICAL
COCKTAIL

Next time you see exotic stems such as these in your florist's shop you will know how to display them with style. The gel crystals not only give support, they also hide the stems and look a bit like crushed ice, too.

TIP
Use miniature edible pineapples on wooden skewers if you cannot get exotic pineapple foliage on stems from your florist.

Fill the pitcher full of florist's crystals in advance so that they have taken up all the water and provide a firm base for the arrangement. Arrange the strelitzias, cutting them to a variety of heights and making sure that their striking flower heads are in profile and clearly visible. Leave room at the front to feature the exotic pineapples. Use the strelitzia leaves to form a background (you can wire these, using the same method as wiring ivy leaves on page 56, so that they can be shaped). Add the mimosa and orchids to finish off.

*b*REAKFAST *e*XTRA

This delicate little arrangement uses a simple cream-colored egg cup and is just the thing for a bedside table or a breakfast tray! The lilies-of-the-valley have a heady scent ~ a lovely perfume for a bedroom.

YOU WILL NEED:

Egg cup

Floral foam

Approximately 12 stems bear grass

9 stems lily-of-the-valley foliage

10 pink sweet peas

13 stems lily-of-the-valley

TIP
If you cannot get sweet peas, use soft pink alstroemerias instead.

Cut the foam so that it extends about 2 inches above rim of the egg cup, and force it into the cup. Define the outline with bear grass, bending one or two stems to bring the arrangement into the center. Follow these lines with the lily-of-the-valley foliage, bringing it slightly forwards into the center. Add the sweet peas, maintaining a bias to the bottom left, and then position the lilies-of-the-valley evenly throughout to finish off.

tulip time

Tulips can either be part of an exotic mix or used on their own. Here they complement the rustic pot to make a fresh and naive arrangement for spring – a perfect way of bringing some fresh color into your home after winter.

YOU WILL NEED:

Large rustic bowl

20 white tulips

20 yellow tulips (we used a variety with multiple blooms per stem)

10 pieces eucalyptus

TIP
Tulips continue to grow after they are cut. Trim off all the white section of the stem before you arrange them and try to position the arrangement in even light. You may need to turn the container during the day.

Put 2–3 inches water in the bottom of the container. Trim all but one of the leaves from each of the tulip stems and place all one color around, starting at the bottom and working your way up. As you add more stems, they support each other. Add the second color towards the center and top of the arrangement, and use the eucalyptus foliage for contrast. Use additional tulip leaves if necessary to hold the shape.

⅁RESSED ℘ALM

The foliage of this palm is almost identical in shape to the foliage on the lilies, and will fool the eye into thinking that it is part of the same plant. If you have a suitable cachepot then you do not need to repot the plant in a vase.

YOU WILL NEED:

Vase or pot

Floral foam

1 tall parlor palm

Spray leaf shine

3 stems lilies (we used 'Star Gazer')

Repot the palm into the vase or a larger container with a wedge of floral foam, placing it as near to the center as possible. Treat the leaves to leaf shine for a fresh, glossy finish. Add lilies so that the stems are close to the stem of the palm, and so that the palm leaves pass either side of the flower stems. Vary the lengths of the stems, then fill in around the base with foliage from the cut stems and one or two open flowers.

TIP
Remember to water lightly every day to keep both the palm and the floral foam damp.

*p*OT ET *f*LEUR

Although it is time consuming to create, this combination of potted plants and cut flowers would be a dramatic addition to a conservatory. The quantity of filler you need will depend on the size of the tank, but it is certain to take more than you think it will.

YOU WILL NEED:
Large glass tank
Dyed statice flowers
Reindeer moss
Potting compost
Clay pebbles
1 guzmania
1 kalanchoe
4 stems butcher's broom
2 stems asters
2 stems monkshood
1 stem Chinese lanterns
Florist's ribbon

Build up the first two layers of pebbles, statice, and moss around the outside of the tank, then fill in the center with potting compost. Remove the plants from their pots and add one in the center and one at one end. Continue the layering to the top, finishing with a layer of pebbles. Add the cut flowers to the bare end of the tank, arranging some foliage and Chinese lanterns through the plants, too. Finish off with two florist's bows (see page 24).

ƒIREPLACE ƒEATURE

Filling a summer fireplace can be difficult, and displays often end up overpowering the space rather than enhancing it. Place this elegant combination of delphiniums and gladioli on the hearth rather than deep into the grate, and it will be sure to create a light focal point for your room once more.

YOU WILL NEED:

Large, tall container

Floral foam

5 stems white gladioli

5 stems delphiniums

5 golden calla lilies

1 stem milkweed

1 stem prairie gentian

2 wired pine cones

3 stems bay

10 stems timothy grass (cattails)

10 stems graminae grass

Fill the container with floral foam so that the top block is tight in the neck but extends about 3 inches above the rim. Position the tall stems of gladioli and delphinium first, using them to make a tall fan shape at the back, with two cut-down gladioli at the sides. Add the lilies, the milkweed, divided in two, and the prairie gentian, divided in three, to the front, leaving space for the pine cones at the very front. Fill in with pieces of bay, stems of timothy grass, and the graminae grass.

*p*LANTED *b*ASKET

Simple in principle but less easy to do well in practice, this planted basket has great elegance of shape and balance, with height at the back and trailing ivy to the front. It will last forever if it is cared for well, and it is a wonderful way of having color in your home all year round.

YOU WILL NEED:

10-inch lined basket

1 large dieffenbachia

1 azalea

1 spider plant, broken into 3

1 trailing ivy, broken into 3

You may need additional soil and sphagnum moss

Remove all the plants from their pots. Place the dieffenbachia at the back of the basket, with the azalea at the front, then fill in with the split spider plant and the ivy. Cover any soil that is visible with sphagnum moss.

TIP
This would be a lovely gift for someone who has not got time to care for cut flowers — new parents, perhaps — or for someone in the hospital.

78

ᴅɪʀᴇᴄᴛᴏʀʏ ᴏꜰ ꜰʟᴏᴡᴇʀꜱ ᴀɴᴅ ꜰᴏʟɪᴀɢᴇ

Botanical name	Common name(s)
Acacia dealbata	Mimosa, silver wattle
Aconitum napellus	Monkshood, helmet flower
Allium sphaerocephalon . . .	Allium, onion head
Alstroemeria hybrids . . .	Alstroemeria, Peruvian lily
Ananas hybrids	Red pineapple, wild pineapple
Anemone coronaria	Anemone, windflower
Anthurium andreanum . . .	Anthurium, tail flower, painter's palette
Antirrhinum majus hybrids . .	Snapdragon
Arachniodes adiantiformus . . .	Heather leaf, leather fern
Asclepias incarnata	Milkweed
Asparagus setaceus . . . . . . (A. plumosus)	Asparagus fern
Aster ericoides	Aster, Michaelmas daisy
Aster novi-belgii	Aster, Michaelmas daisy
Buxus sempervirens	Box, common box
Calamagrostis canescens	Purple small-reed
Calendula officinalis	Marigold
Callistephus chinensis hybrids .	China aster
Calluna spp.	Heather
Carthamus tinctorius	Safflower, dyer's saffron, false saffron
Centaurea cyanus	Cornflower, bluebottle, knapweed
Centaurea dealbata	Cornflower, bluebottle, knapweed
Chamaedorea elegans . . . . (Neanthe bella)	Parlor palm, dwarf mountain palm
Chlorophytum comosum . . . . (C. capense)	Spider plant
Chrysanthemum hybrids . . .	Chrysanthemum
Cladonia rangiferina	Reindeer moss
Convallaria majalis	Lily-of-the-valley
Craspedia globosa	Craspedia
Cymbidium hybrids	Orchid
Daboecia spp.	Heather
Dahlia hybrids	Dahlia
Dasylirion texanum	Bear grass
Delphinium elatum hybrids . .	Delphinium
Dendrobium hybrids	Orchid
Dianthus spp.	Carnation, pink
Dieffenbachia varieties	Dieffenbachia, dumb cane, leopard lily
Erica spp.	Heather
Eucalyptus gunnii	Eucalyptus, cider gum
Euonymus fortunei . . . . . 'Emerald and Gold'	Euonymus
Euphorbia fulgens	Euphorbia, spurge
Eustoma grandiflorum . . . . (Lisianthus russellianus)	Prairie gentian
Fagus sylvatica	Beech
Freesia hybrids	Freesia

Botanical name	Common name(s)
Gentiana hybrids	Gentian
Gerbera jamesonii	Gerbera Barberton daisy, Transvaal daisy
Gladiolus hybrids	Gladiolus, sword lily
Graminae	Ken grass
Guzmania hybrid	Guzmania, orange star
Gypsophila paniculata	Baby's breath
Hedera helix	Ivy
Helianthus annus	Sunflower
Iris spp.	Iris
Jasminum officinale	Jasmine, jessamine
Kalanchoe blossfeldiana . . .	Kalanchoe, flaming Katy
Lathyrus odoratus	Sweet pea
Laurus nobilis	Bay
Liatris spicata (l. callilepis) . .	Liatris, gay feather, blazing star
Lilium hybrids	Lily
Lilium lancifolium . . . . . (l. tigrinum)	Tiger lily
Lilium longifolium	White trumpet lily, Easter lily, Bermuda lily
Limonium sinuatum	Statice
Luzula sylvatica	Greater woodrush
Nigella damascena	Love-in-a-mist, nigella
Ornithogalum arabicum	Star of Bethlehem
Physalis alkekengi franchetii . .	Chinese lantern, bladder cherry, winter cherry
Polianthes tuberosa	Tuberose
Protea spp.	Protea
Prunus laurocerasus	Laurel, cherry laurel
Reseda lutea	Wild mignonette
Rhododendron azara	Azalea
Rosa hybrids	Rose
Rosmarinus officinalis	Rosemary
Ruscus aculeatus	Butcher's broom
Salix matsudana 'Tortuosa' . .	Dragon's claw willow, contorted willow
Scabiosa caucasica hybrids . .	Scabious
Sphagnum spp.	Sphagnum moss
Strelitzia reginae	Strelitzia, bird-of-paradise flower
Symphoricarpos albus	Snowberry
Trachelium caeruleum	Throatwort
Tsuga canadensis	Sugar pine, Canada hemlock, eastern hemlock
Tulipa spp.	Tulip
Typha latifolia	Bulrush/reed mace
Veronica longifolia	Veronica, spiked speedwell
Zantedeschia aethiopica	Arum lily
Zantedeschia elliottiana and rehmanii hybrids	Golden arum lily, calla lily

INDEX